EVOLVE

THE NEW RULES FOR ~~SECURITY~~ CAREER

WILL ROWE

Copyright © 2017 by Will Rowe.

Follow me on twitter @MSFTrecruit

Connect with me on LinkedIn

WHY I WROTE THIS BOOK

Firstly, thank you for buying this book.

Let me be clear on something however: this is not a book full of tips and tricks on how to ace interviews and negotiate the highest possible salary. This is about the most important job in the world: yours.

And furthermore it is about you personally and your journey throughout your career, through the ups and downs and cock ups and successes.

So: you can stop reading now if you like. It's fine. I understand.

I get it.

This is going to take time and some effort. Not everybody is at the point where they are looking to do that.

THE GOOD OLD DAYS OF FINDING A JOB.

Historically, finding a job was as easy as answering an advert in the printed press or on Jobserve or Monster. Going back 20 years, the IT industry was significantly smaller with a lot less products and also with a lot fewer people working in it. This meant fewer respondents per advert, and headhunters had to work via referrals more with a bit of mapping of IT departments on the side.

Getting a phone call from a headhunter was something quite flattering for many people.

You would send your résumé into a company having seen an advert, get a phone call inviting you for an interview, and after a couple of meetings would either get the job or not. You might get rejected but it was a very transactional arrangement: I have a job, you want a job, let's do this.

We didn't have social media. We didn't have the internet really. We had adverts and newspapers and an IT industry who were doing more with online job boards and who were putting their résumés onto them and waiting for people to call them.

Fast forward to now: We have social media: LinkedIn, Facebook, Twitter, Instagram, Xing. We have more online job boards than I can write here. Everyone is online and their details are as well. We have blogging, GitHub, Stack Overflow, Youtube celebrities, memes, and it is crazy how much noise is out there now.

I wrote this book because things have changed significantly and I haven't even discussed the IT vendor space. In today's world it isn't enough to just apply for jobs any more: the best jobs are going to those who apply the principles of 'Pull Marketing' to their own careers.

The rules have changed.

Let's look what you need to do to evolve yourself to take advantage of this.

TABLE OF CONTENTS

Rule 1: Being Happy isn't enough to Evolve.

Let me tell you a story:

I have a good friend called Ray. Ray is one of the best friends that I have, a real stalwart who I've known for over 20 years now.

We first met in 1996 when I was at University in London and was competing for Kingston upon Thames Athletics Club. We bonded over a love of rock climbing, hill walking and beer and within the space of about 3 months had organized a week-long jaunt to the Highlands of Scotland to visit and climb some of the most spectacular mountains in the UK.

Ray was working for a payroll company at the time and to my eyes had it all: company car, a salary (hey - I was at Uni!) and was travelling up and down the UK visiting far and exotic places like Hull, Peterborough and Berwick upon Tweed on a regular basis.

The product ran on DOS (I didn't know this then) and Windows NT3.5.

Fast forward 5 years to 2001 and I had been working for an IT recruitment company for about 2 years. We were into the Dotcom bubble, Windows 2000 had been released, I had learned how to send an email, and I picked up a role in IT support that was looking for someone with a solid technical background who could talk with customers and fix issues.

I picked up the phone and called Ray (with a little trepidation - we were into new territory for our friendship here) to find out if he might be interested.

He wasn't.

Ray was happy where he was, and the product he was supporting was being upgraded to work on Windows NT4.

A few more years passed, and I dropped another role in front of him which he interviewed for, was offered but ultimately decided that it wasn't time to move on. Windows Server 2003 had been released, but the payroll software he supported was still on NT4.

A few more years passed and I put a new role in front of him. Again he interviewed, again he got an offer from them, and again he decided to stay where he was.

The product hadn't changed much, was still primarily DOS based and was sitting on Windows Server 2000. This was now 2006, and the Operating System was 6 years old.

Each of the roles I had positioned him for would have allowed him to upskill and update his technical experience.

The product he was supporting was now so far behind the curve that it was in danger of becoming obsolete. Ray was now part of the furniture - he had been with the company for 15 years - he was sitting in a support manager's job managing a junior team that kept leaving to work on more up to date and sexy tech and his technical skills were out of date by about 4-5 years.

Ray, like many people I speak with the in the industry, was happy. If you can be happy in your job then the world is a great place.

Think about it: we are told all through our lives that personal happiness, in one form or another, is what we should be aiming for.

The challenge that Ray was facing was that although he was happy he wasn't thinking about his career beyond where he was right then and that is the hardest thing to do. Although he knew the product he was supporting inside and out, nobody in 2006 was hiring for Windows Server 2000 and DOS support skills and the software he worked with was so bespoke as to be unheard of by many people.

Ray had, quite inadvertently and by doing absolutely nothing wrong, found himself in a Career Cul-de-Sac.

WHAT IS A CAREER CUL-DE-SAC?

A Career Cul-de-Sac is not a dead-end. A dead-end is a scary place, and you feel like you need to turn around and get the hell back to a place that lets you go somewhere. It has the word 'Dead' in it, and that is a bad word for where we are at.

"Shit, honey! I've taken a wrong turn in my career and hit a dead-end. I've got to do something!"

A Career Cul-de-Sac is far more insidious than that, and far more deadly.

People actually like living in a Career Cul-de-Sac. They are comfortable, happy, the bills get paid and they have the respect of their peers.

And like Ray the world passes them by until they wake up one day and realise that something just isn't quite right: they have become obsolete without even realising it. The BBQs and the socialising in number 1 Career Cul-de-Sac have been great and in many other industries this would have set that person up for life: the IT industry is one of the most competitive and brutal in the world. If Charles Darwin were alive today he would not be writing about the Galapagos Islands he would be pointing at the Tech scene and shouting "Look! I was right!! Right there – look!" Only those who are able to evolve to keep pace with it survive.

Evolve or Die.

So.

HOW OFTEN DO WE FIND OURSELVES IN A CAREER CUL-DE-SAC?

All the time. Like - all the time.

Your average person (and by that I mean pretty much everyone) who is in a permanent role only really thinks about changing jobs when they are either a) bored, b) pissed off, c) bored and pissed off. It is different if you are a contractor because of the transient nature of the role that you do - if you are bored then the contract will be up at some point anyway forcing you to make a decision. That being said, contractors and interims need to evolve even faster than permanent employees to defend their income levels and stay relevant.

Rule 2: Evolve through a Career Audit

Ask yourself: when was the last time you gave your current role and career a serious audit.

Where is your career actually going? Do you know? Do you care?

Are you happy, and if you are happy is it at the expense of finding yourself in a Career Cul-de-Sac?

Being happy in your role is now not enough for the long or even medium term. IT doesn't have a medium/long term any more...

For Ray, the pace of technological change had left him behind in a role which was only applicable to one tiny specific product and industry.

Technology is moving faster at this point than at any time in history. Look at Microsoft Teams: this went from an idea to being Generally Available in a matter of months: previously it would have taken years.

It is this pace of change that is going to be the biggest challenge to IT people everywhere whether they are permanent or contract employees.

The most fundamental realization for many in recent years is that the technology they started working with at the beginning of their career is not the one they will finish with. This might seem like a no brainier to many of you reading this, but this was not something that the older generations really figured on when they were working with AS400 and COBOL in the 90's and 2000's.

My view is that every role you take needs to enhance your skill set and leave you better off at the end of it. The average person in IT in a permanent role stays with an employer for 2 years and yet technology is moving faster than this now. It has become increasingly apparent to me that with the pace of change in the industry an IT Pro's role is not their day job: their role is now to keep up to date and relevant to the broader market. If your employer is not giving you this you need to start thinking about making a change.

If you are contracting what are the projects you are working on right now? Are they keeping you current? You are ultimately responsible for your own training and development: when was the last time you put yourself through a training course that might shift your experience into a slightly new track?

Everybody in IT needs to be thinking about their next role, and their relevance to the market moving forwards. Most people I speak to are aware of this in a vague way, but few actually do anything about it until they are seriously bored or they have thrown up in the punch at the Christmas Party and are looking for a swift exit.

How do I give myself a Career Audit, and will it hurt?

I believe that you need to perform a Career Audit every 6 months or so. It shouldn't hurt more than any other personal examination you have given yourself, and should provide you with some insights that allow you to answer the big question: do I need to take action now?

Start with your current role and situation.

Ask yourself this:

Role

- What is my current role?
- Am I enjoying it? (Remember – this is not enough anymore!)
- Is there a career path available to me in my current role? Do I want to go in that direction?
- Do I understand how to get my next pay rise and promotion?

Tech

- What technologies am I working with currently?
- Which versions?
- How up to date are these in comparison to the rest of the market i.e. how many releases behind are you?
- What projects am I working on and what is coming up?
- Will I be able to get onto those projects?

Personal Development

- What was the last training I did?
- When was the last training?
- Was there an industry certification at the end of it?
- Was it in something that benefits me or is it just benefiting my employer?
- When is my next training booked?

The Broader Industry:

- What are the current trends in your market?
- What is the noise on Social Media about new tech, new releases and versions within your area of expertise?
- Most importantly, is there a fundamental shift coming up in your industry? If so, what do you need to do to be a part of it?

Let me give you an example of this.

I have been writing and blogging recently about how the Microsoft Skype for Business market is changing currently from a predominantly on-premises solution to a cloud-based model via Office 365; about how this will affect those people who do not look to upskill in the broader O365 space and pick up those all-important cloud-based skills. It has been and still is a very niche space, with good salaries and contract rates for those Architects, Consultants and Engineers who work within it.

There is an industry shift coming and those working within need to be aware of this and evolve their skill-set into what the market will be demanding in the next few years. If they cannot do this and get ahead of it they will be left behind.

Because of this change it is putting pressure on them to make some tough decisions: they need to cross-train and develop and if they are not getting those skills which will keep them relevant then it is a big fat 'Yes I need to take action now!" moment.

An employer views your job as a function to develop their software tool, or look after their infrastructure, or manage their projects so that they can make money. It is often a philosophy directly at odds with what you need to be doing.

Remember: Evolve or Die.

DO YOU NEED TO TAKE ACTION?

RULE 3: EVOLVE BY KNOWING WHAT YOU WANT.

I am a recruiter / headhunter / architect of people's destiny / messenger of opportunity. I have been finding people jobs in the tech space for the best part of 18 years and have placed people with pretty much every skill set you might imagine in this time.

In 2001 I once went out and found someone from just having their name and a company they worked for 8 years previously. Sounds easy? No LinkedIn or Social Media back then. The Internet was basically porn, and very distracting. No information online about anything. Still sound easy?

So - I like to think I'm pretty good at what I do. Please don't send me emails disabusing me of that notion.

The thing is; it's not about me. It's about you.

I could have the best job in the world sat waiting for you, but if you don't want it then it is not the best job in the world. I might believe it is the right fit for you but if you are not interested my belief doesn't matter.

So, I'll ask again: what do you want?

If you cannot articulate it then it is best to take some time figuring it out. I (and my brethren in the recruitment world) need some guidance from you about what we are going to look for.

It is absolutely fine, however, to ask us what we think that you should be doing next and what your options are moving: I get that a lot.

BUILDING A TEMPLATE FOR YOUR NEW ROLE.

Have you ever sat down and really thought about where you are going and what you would like to be doing? Do you know what the career paths available to you are from your current role?

If you don't know where you want to go, how can you go there? That being said you might not know where you want to go, so we can start to design your ideal Job Description. You can use many of the answers to the questions in Career Audit to help with this.

Take out a tablet or notebook. Or (crazy, I know!) a pen or paper, ask yourself the following questions and write down the answers:

1. What is my current role?
2. What are the duties I undertake within it?
3. How do I feel about the Location? Does it need to change?
4. How do I feel about my Remuneration? What do I want next?

5. What duties do I enjoy doing now in my current role? (As many as you can)

6. What duties don't I enjoy doing now in my current role? (As many as you can)

7. What 3 things do I want to do more of?

8. What 3 things do I want to do less of?

9. What sort of company do I want to work for next?

10. What role would I like to do next?

11. What does somebody doing that role currently do that I do not?

12. What do I want learn about next?

Use the answers as follows in the template below:

- Answers to questions 3, 4, 5, 7, 9 & 10 give you the duties of your new role, the location & package you want to look at, and the kind of company you would like to work for.
- Answers to questions 6 & 8 identify what you want to actively change.
- Answers to questions 11 allow you to start to identify gaps in your skill set, and 12 will let you begin to list how to bridge that gap with new training.

TEMPLATE FOR YOUR IDEAL NEW ROLE

Job Title:

Location:

Salary:

Type of Company / Ideal Company:

Day to Day Duties:

Use the answers to questions 3, 4, 5, 7, 9 & 10 to build these

What do I want to Change?

Answers to questions 6 & 8 identify what you want to actively change

Training opportunities & opportunities for advancement

Answers to questions 11 allow you to start to identify gaps in your skill set, and 12 will let you begin to list new training areas.

What is important to me in a new employer?

Based on your Values – see next section

WHAT IS IMPORTANT TO YOU IN A NEW EMPLOYER?

There are these things called Values which we all have within us. They are what we believe and tie in quite closely with our morals.

When I ask someone what they want to do next, 99% of the time they talk about the next role they want, and less often about the things that they want to learn. They talk about the day to day duties of the job, the location, salary etc.

When I ask someone "What is important to you in a new employer?" they come back with a very different response. This is because this question speaks directly to their Values: usually I hear something along the lines of "Empowered working" or 'Treats me with respect" or "A culture where you can learn without micro-management"

This is very different to a job and yet it is often more important to some people to find an employer whose Values align with theirs than it is to get that extra bump in salary.

Why do people stay with an organization for longer than the average 2 years that we see in the industry? It is, in my opinion, because they find an employer / manager who believe in treating people in a way that ties in with the answers to the above question.

Conversely, when discussing a new role with a hiring manager I will ask them "what is important to you in a new hire?" The answers again are very different to career history and skills and experience: they are about the kind of person they want and what their Values are.

So: take out that tablet or notebook again. Write down the first things that come into your head in response to this:

What is important to you in a new employer?

Write it down.

Keep going.

Now - put that with the other answers in your Ideal Job Description. You should now have a decent template of what your new role might look like: now you need to find it.

Let me stress this: if your current role and employer can offer you the career path and training that you want, and have a similar set of Values to yours then you are set up and don't need to make a change.

If you unsure where you can go within your current role or what the training options are available to you then you can have these discussions with your employer to cover what you want to be doing (at an appraisal or pay review, for example) This will then give you the knowledge to judge whether you are in a Career cul-de-sac so that you can make a decision to get out of it.

Rule 4: Evolve and be found.

The world of Recruitment has changed significantly over the past five years: most large organizations have adopted an internal Talent Acquisition process or have signed agreements that allow an RPO (Recruitment Process Outsourcing) organization to handle their recruitment for them. With the rise of LinkedIn, Xing, (mostly used in Germany) GitHub and many of the other Social platforms which seem to come and go with a bewildering speed it has meant that getting access to people has become much simpler. Why pay a recruiter a 20% margin or fee for someone when they can pay a salary to a recruiter turned gamekeeper and make multiple hires at a fraction of the cost?

What the top people in the industry that I talk to do to set them apart is demonstrate their knowledge. As my old Maths teacher used to say (in frequently shouty and exasperated tones) "Show your working!"

If you are a Developer get your work up on Stack Overflow or GitHub. If you are an Infrastructure specialist start a blog showing cases where you have seen issues crop up that you have overcome – obviously keep an eye out to protect company IP and secrets!

Why is this important?

Employers and recruiters see résumés all day. A Talent Acquisition person looking to fill a role might see in excess of 100 résumés per role and when they have up to 40 roles on at a time you can see how this becomes a challenge. If you can show how your experience is better / deeper / more relevant then you are likely to be put to the front of the queue.

Recently I was looking for a User Adoption Specialist who could train users on SharePoint for a migration project to O365. I was looking through résumés when I came across one with a link to a blog placed prominently at the top of the first page.

I clicked it, and the first posting I saw was entitled "What do you need to know when training users on SharePoint in O365?"

This person got the role, and is still on contract with the customer as I write this. It was not just the blog posting that did it, but the employer was in a tight spot and the fact that there was a blog demonstrating how the person worked just backed up what was said in interview and reinforced the fact this is a low risk option for them.

This all takes time, however, and it is worth working this into a plan well in advance of moving on. If you are a contractor then I believe that having something like this going along in the background will only increase your ability to charge a premium as you are perceived to be more of a specialist in your chosen area.

IT'S ALL ABOUT THE SEARCH ENGINE OPTIMIZATION.

In today's world of massive data-obesity how do you get found for a new role when you do start looking? Sadly it isn't about being the best at what you do anymore: you need to understand how the world of recruitment finds people.

Every job board that you I can think of (Monster, Jobserve, Jobsite, Dice, Reed, TotalJobs, Careers4A etc) has their own search engine for when rugged recruiters such as myself log in and type in an elegant Boolean Search string. The résumés that come back are in the order of most relevant rather than date-wise. Relevance is based on the number of key terms in the résumé that match the search, and the most relevant are the ones with the most number of repetitions in them. This is the same for the internal CRMs, Applicant Tracking Systems and recruitment databases that companies own and work with.

WHAT DOES THIS MEAN FOR YOU?

If you are not optimizing your résumé with the key terms that a recruiter might search on then you are not going to be top of the list. More importantly, if you are not repeating those key terms then the Search Engine will prioritize other people over you.

Question: Where do you hide a body where no-one will ever find it?

Answer: Page 4 of Google.

If I'm searching for someone to fill a role against a deadline, and I speak to 5 people who are right for it the then I will generally stop after this at I don't want to send too many people and swamp the hiring manager. If those 5 people are on the first page of results then I will not be going through the remaining pages of a 100 person set of results and reading the résumés just in case.

How do you optimize a résumé so that it doesn't read like list of repeated skills?

The simplest way to optimize your résumé is by using the following technique.

Building Silos of Information:

Go back to that notebook / tablet / pen & paper.

Write down the top 3-5 technical skills you have. If you are a non-technical person such as a Project / Programme Manager then this works as well for your skill set.

Write down the skill, the versions of that skill, and what you have been doing with it.

E.g - Messaging: Exchange 2010 - 2016.

- Exchange 2010: Design and implementation of solutions for up to 5,000 seats.
- Exchange 2013: Design and implementation of solutions, migrations of users to Exchange 2013.
- Exchange 2016 - Migrations of on-prem / hybrid solutions to Exchange 2016 and O365.

Do it for the next ones until you have a page with this filled out.

What you have here now is a ready to go template that can be put into your résumé which does a couple of things:

1) It bulks up significantly the SEO of your experience.

2) It gives your friendly recruiter-extraordinaire or hiring manager some context for your skills as well.

Please, please be aware that if your whole résumé is written like this it will put people off. Use your discretion, and consider what role you are looking to do next before just doing a brain dump of your skills and putting them in your résumé (more about tailoring your résumé later) You might not actually need to use all 5 of your main tech skill sets in your résumé and if you want to hedge your bets then put it on the last page of your experience.

Question: Where do you bury a set of skills where no-one will ever find them?

Answer: The last page of your résumé.

JOB TITLES ARE BULLSHIT: IS YOURS?

Think of the job titles that recruiters will be searching for because these are also SEO-able. I have seen some truly horrific job titles in my life, from something like "DSV L2 Engineer" to "IT Consultant".

I will always remember my first manager in recruitment, a top man called Jake King who now runs his own agency called Ambis focused on the Accounting Software market. He hired me in the September of 1999 after seeing my unbridled need for a job which paid a base salary and me basically begging for a chance to do "the recruitment".

On our very first day, Jake said something that has always stuck with me: "Will," he said, leaning forward on the board room table to look me in the eye, "There is one thing and one thing only that you need to know about job titles in IT. They are all bullshit."

Think about it.

I know an IT Manager who manages a team of 18 through 3 Team Leaders for a global management consultancy. I also know an IT Manager who is the sole IT support person for a small 75-man business who runs half a dozen servers and who has just moved the company over to O365. What is the difference between a Junior Developer and a Developer? Seniority? Fine. But really, what is the actual difference?

Which one is correct? Which one describes the other person more accurately? They both do. The term IT Consultant is without doubt the worst possible Job Title in existence: what exactly does a Consultant do? I have asked many people down the years and they all have a slightly different take on it.

Job titles are bullshit. Jake's job title is now "King of Recruitment" so I don't think that it is only the IT industry where this is prevalent.

Now - having said that you need to have some sort of a job title down so if it describes your role then perfect: more importantly if it happens to match titles with the role you are applying for then even better. It might be better to give your actual title and then if it is generic / vague you can always put something afterwards that describes it more effectively:

IT Manager (Systems & Server Manager)

Don't go crazy and make things up though. In all likelihood you will be asked for a reference from that role and if you are saying you were the CTO and you looked after 5 desktops and the office dog you will get found out...

Rule 5: Evolve and Sell.

Your résumé

What is the purpose of a résumé? Can anyone tell me? It is not the following:

- To show your career history.
- To list your achievements.
- A chance to showcase your love of extra-curricular activities.
- An opportunity to explain that you work equally well as part of a team or on your own.
- To explain that you have 'excellant communication skills' (and yes – I know this is spelled incorrectly – it is a direct quote! Oh the irony...)

The purpose of a résumé is quite simple and when you are putting yours together and writing it you need to bear this in mind: the purpose of a résumé is to effectively sell your experience and to get you an interview.

Let's think about that: the purpose of your résumé is to get you an interview, and to effectively sell your skills and experience.

It does not need to be a work of genius or a work of art. It just needs to get your skills across to an interviewer so that they want to meet with you.

Remember: a résumé's purpose is to effectively sell your experience and to get you an interview. If yours does not do this, then you need to think long and hard about changing it. Actually - don't think long and hard. Just change it.

"AVOID EMPLOYING UNLUCKY PEOPLE - THROW HALF OF THE PILE OF RÉSUMÉS IN THE BIN WITHOUT READING THEM."
David Brent

HOW TO SELL IN A RÉSUMÉ WITHOUT APPEARING TO DO ANYTHING.

If the purpose of a résumé is to effectively sell you and you are not a salesperson, then how do you go about it? I speak to so many people and they understand on some level that they need to sell themselves but they have never been told how to do that.

Let me show you how.

At the most fundamental and basic level, selling something is very easy. You need to identify what somebody wants and then deliver it to them. Nothing more; nothing less.

Identify & Deliver. That's it.

Let's think about this: you walk on to a car lot and a good salesperson asks you what you are looking for, what kind of mileage, size, usage, engine specs, cost etc... They then steer you towards the vehicle that best matches your budget and then onto the ones that you can't afford but which match your requirements. And then there is the age-old tussle of finding a vehicle which is the compromise that you can live with. Or do what I do: see the prettiest car, throw caution to the wind and believe them when they say that it isn't about the overall cost of the car but your ability to meet the repayments, and don't you just look so 'right' sitting in the driver's seat. A test drive? Of course, sir... And will the lady be attending? She's just settling the divorce proceedings. I see, sir... Excellent.

OK - I might have some issues to work out but it was a very, very nice car.

The Hiring Manager is the person you need to sell to. They have a set of requirements (key skills and experiences) that they want, and you need to deliver them. Simple.

TAILORING YOUR EXPERIENCE.

Every role is different. Every person is different. Every person's skills and experience are different. Each role has differences based upon the environment or the project or the day to day duties.

Consider this: none of your experience matters to a hiring manager as much as the requirements of the job. They are hiring for a specific skill set and person, and your résumé needs to reflect this.

My strongest advice when applying for a new role is to look at the Job Description / Advertisement and identify the key skills that are required. If in doubt, call the recruiter / company and ask to speak to someone about it prior to applying. I would personally explain why you are doing this, and that you are looking to bring out in your résumé the key areas of relevance. If you cannot speak with someone then you will need to draw some conclusions from the JD / Ad. Highlight some of the key skills, look at your résumé: does it effectively sell your experience?

Most résumés that cross my desk need some work prior to sending them to the employer. This work usually entails getting more information in the form of a 'brain dump' on a specific subject and will be with the express purpose of bringing out in the résumé the things that are most relevant to the role.

THE BRAIN DUMP

This aptly named term does just what it says on the tin.

If your résumé is coming up light in a certain area DO NOT do a re-write of the résumé at this time. You will spend more time worrying about the look, feel and format of the thing than on the quality of the information.

Open a blank email. I always recommend an email as I personally find a blank Word document a little intimidating sometimes and I just don't know where to begin. We are so used to writing emails though that it is almost an ingrained behavior and we are able to start much more easily. How do you think I started writing this?

Now: write down everything that you have done in a specific area that is relevant to the requirements of the job description. You can use the "Silos of Information" technique described above whilst doing this, and it might also be a good idea to put down some specific projects or experiences that showcase your obvious expertise in this area. Make sure that you relate what you have done to which employer - create sub-headings on your email for later.

Once you have done this, stop and reread it. Does it best reflect your skills, or do you need to add more to it? The benefit of putting it down in this format is that you can see your writing without any of the associated flimflammery, puffiness and general dilution that a résumé provides. Here are your skills in condensed form like a shot of good espresso rather than what is often the equivalent of a latte: good coffee poured into about a pint of milk and 'frothed'. And then ruined. Because really, who really likes latte? Come on - just have a hot chocolate and get over yourself.

I digress.

Skills - yes that was it. Take your condensed experience and put it back into the résumé, using the sub-headings to identify what you did for which employer and put it in the relevant place. Why is this important? A good résumé demonstrates not just what you can do, but where you have done it. A recruiter or hiring manager likes to see the skills and the context of them. A list of technical skills on the front page without showing where you have used them tells the person reading it nothing: show them where and how you have used them!

Why do we want to do this? The answer is above, but I'll repeat it for you: the purpose of a résumé is to effectively sell you and get an interview. If an employer is hiring for a specific skill set then that is what they want to see on the résumé, not the myriad other things you have done. The other things are important but secondary to the primary requirements of the job.

One of the biggest challenges you face as a job-seeker is that you will realistically be hired on the past 18-24 months' work and yet many times the quality of information isn't there meaning that you will not get the all-important interview.

THE FIRST PAGE OF YOUR RÉSUMÉ.

The first page should have everything on it that will make a Hiring Manager want to continue reading your résumé. I can, in the space of 4-6 seconds, decide whether I will actually spend the time reading your résumé properly and if you are a person who is worth a call for the role that I have. It sounds ridiculous doesn't it? 4-6 seconds?

Let me break it down for you: I have worked as a Recruitment Consultant for 18 years. Figuring a 240 working day year that is 4,320 days spent doing this job of which each day was conservatively 8 hours per day. That means that I have spent 34,560 hours recruiting IT people into IT jobs.

Wow.

I have only just realized how long that is.

If I work on the assumption that I have looked very conservatively at 40 résumés per day, that means that I have looked at 172,800 résumés in that period of time.

I base my initial skim on the keywords that jump out at me, the number of times that those keywords are in the résumé, the companies that you have worked at and whether you have been doing the right things with the technology that the employer is after. For me it takes 4-6 seconds: many employers will skim a résumé in 30-60 seconds and their initial decision to read on is based on this.

Your résumé needs to stand out and the first page is hugely important in this.

Your front page needs to have:

- Your name
- Your location / address and if you will relocate (if applicable to the role)
- Your Nationality including Visa status (if applicable)
- Whether you have a Driver's License
- Your Current role (as above - not just Job Title – make sure it is descriptive)
- Your notice period from your current role
- Your availability to interview

EDUCATION & CERTIFICATIONS

OK – I'm going to be controversial. Go with me on this, and don't jump to conclusions about anything before you have read the whole piece.

I have a tough question for you: does your Education sell you? Do you have good grades and a Degree / Masters / PhD in a Tech- / Science-related field / any field? Do you have an Apprenticeship which has given you a vocational route into the IT sector?

If so – put it front and center in the résumé.

The same goes for Industry Certifications and Accreditations: how up to date are you? I frequently see certifications on the front page of a résumé that go back to 2003 and sometimes earlier with nothing recent. This does not sell you unless the employer is looking for someone with that (now sadly obsolete) certification.

If (like me) you viewed school and education as something to be endured while focusing on the things that you actually enjoyed (Drama – and before Glee made it cool); had more than a passing acquaintance with detentions and un-submitted homework; got caught writing a poem entitled 'Boredom' during your Biology A-Level which led to a one-sided conversation with the Headmaster regarding just how your iambic pentameter was not as good as you would have hoped, and how your reference to him and his parentage was not as flattering as he would have hoped, then you might have not got the grades that you wanted.

If this is the case then put your Education on the last page. If you have up to date Industry Certifications that show your dedication to your chosen field and School grades that don't then separate them so that the Certs are on the first page and the Education towards the back of the résumé.

If your Certifications are not up to date (and by this I mean more than 3-5 years out of date) then put them on the last page or leave them out entirely. They do not sell you. With the pace of change in the industry you need to be constantly learning and certifying to get that next job and employers want to see that you have the get up and go to be seeking to improve your skills.

If you have a home lab where you test problems or are part of a beta-testing group get it on the résumé. Mention your blog / link to GitHub / Stackoverflow. Show your working on the first page.

Let me be clear on this point: we are not the sum of our education and school grades and if you have any experience in the industry at all then you will know how little that prepares you for the day-to-day work.

Am I saying that you should be ashamed of your grades? Absolutely not. Am I ashamed of my grades? Nope – not even slightly, and they are not great at all in comparison with many of the people I went to school with and have worked with since.

So why put them on the last page?

I refer you to the whole purpose of a résumé which is to effectively sell you and get you an interview: nothing more, nothing less. If your education does not add to the overall positive impression and selling of you then put it somewhere else and focus on filling up that space with experience that matches the key requirements of the role i.e. reasons why you should be interviewed.

MOST PERSONAL SUMMARIES ARE A WASTE OF INK: IS YOURS?

Nearly every résumé I see has a Personal Statement / Summary section. It usually includes something like: "I am an excellent communicator with the ability to work well both in a team and on my own. I am motivated, driven and target oriented and happy to go the extra mile. Blah blah blah, generic phrase, cliché, generic phrase, cliché."

This is the first thing the hiring manager or recruiter sees, and it usually is the first thing to be discounted. It is also the first major missed opportunity to sell you in your résumé, and as such we need to rectify that immediately.

Have a look at your summary / personal statement. What does it say? I'm going to bet that you have one similar to the above, or which has elements of it in there.

Question: what does need to be in the summary then, if the usual fluff isn't correct?

Answer: detail around whatever you have done that matches the requirements of the role.

If the Job Description asks for experience of the following:

- iOS Architecture
- Azure or AWS
- Swift Native Development: Objective-C is nice to have.
- SSO experience designing mobile apps that use Single Sign On
- Analytics – have worked with Google Analytics and Flurry, Crashalytics is useful.

Then your summary should reflect your experiences in this space along the lines of:

"I am an iOS Lead Developer with strong experience architecting and developing solutions on the iOS platform. I have development skills using native SWIFT and Objective-C, with extensive experience developing secure applications that use SSO products like Shibboleth, Keychain and Centrify.

Recently I worked on a project at a major financial institution where we were creating secure mobile applications on Azure PaaS, building new features using Adobe Analytics."

Note that this brings out as many of the key skills from the Job Description as possible, and if it is on the first page of your résumé it will immediately catch the attention of the person reading it.

The Body of the Résumé.

The body of the résumé is your career history and is the point where you tell the story of your work experience, who you have worked for, what you did and what your duties and achievements were.

You need to remember that you still need to be selling in the main part of your résumé. If you have a first page which fulfils the criteria of the requirements of the role, talks about the things that they really want know about and gets the hiring manager or recruiter frothing at the mouth with excitement but you don't back it up and provide context in the subsequent career history then you will find yourself in at best the 'Maybe' pile and at worst 'File 13' or the bin that David Brent so enjoyed talking about earlier. If you have specific experience in a skill set or technology that someone is looking for, get it into your career history. Be specific. Tailor your experience to fit the requirements of the role as shown above and use the 'Building Silos of Information' technique if you are struggling.

Put your experience in reverse chronological order (Current company first, going backwards) and make sure that the last 2-3 years of experience has enough detail to show what you have done, with less information the further back you go. If you have been working prior to the year 2000 then I would stop there and write

"Experience prior to 2000 available upon request" as it was 17.5 years ago at the point of writing this and now not relevant to the role you are applying for. You could almost do this for anything prior to 2005 as long as the later experience sells you into the new opportunity.

This is a valuable thing to use if your résumé is starting to run on.

The 2-page résumé

Unless you are a well-known CEO-Level person then steer away from a 2-page résumé. It is absolutely fine if you have not had enough experience to actually fill a couple of pages but please for the love of all that is good, stop trying to condense your experience down into a couple of sides of A4.

I want you to promise me something: the next time someone tells you that you should be putting your 5-10 years+ of experience in 2 pages I'd like you to tell them politely to go and fuck off, and when they get there to go and fuck off again. These people know nothing about you, your skills, your experience, and for some reason they want you to condense your career history into a format which gives no depth whatsoever.

Anyone who tells you to use a 2-page résumé is setting you up to fail. Seriously.

If you have 3-4 pages of relevant experience, then put it down. If you have 5-6 pages then that is OK, but try not to let things go any further than that - 6 pages are a loooong document.

Show your projects, demonstrate your skills and make sure that you put in enough detail to ensure that whoever is reading the document feels that you have the experience to warrant an interview.

When a well written, tailored résumé hit's the desk of a Hiring Manager it stands out above the rest. Period.

The 1-page Résumé

No. Don't do it. Just don't.

I had a sales person send me his résumé, which was one page. Just one. Not two pages. Just one. It said nothing really about his experience, his achievements in any real detail, or really anything that would make me want to call him, let alone an employer with a burning desire to hire.

He also included a motivational life philosophy he lives by: "Go for the moon. if you don't get it at least you'll still be heading for the stars" and a pie chart of his day (excerpts from this involve "sleeping like a baby" and "settling in on the sofa for whatever Sky decides to throw at us") Poor grammar aside, this is like a page right out of David Brent's résumé, and as such it does not effectively sell that candidate's experience to really any role I can think of as there is no real detail there. I later realised that it was based on Marissa Mayer's résumé which was bad when she did it, and awful when he did.

So – 1-page résumés are out. So are 2-page résumés.

To recap:

- The purpose of a résumé is to effectively sell you and get you an interview.
- Selling is where you identify what someone wants and then you give it them.
- You can build out your experience using the 'Brain Dump' & 'Building Silos of Information' techniques.
- Job Titles are Bullshit.
- You will need to tailor your résumé at times to best reflect your experience in relation to a specific role.
- This extra information will also help make your résumé more findable by bulking up the Search Engine Optimization of it.
- Upload your new résumé to a range of Job Boards (Monster, Jobserve etc...)

Rule 6: Evolve your Brand

Social footprint

It isn't just on a résumé that you need to think about SEO. LinkedIn is by far and away the best networking site for being found for a new role currently in my opinion. Think about the keywords that recruiters will be searching on (skills etc) and get some repetitions going on your profile.

LinkedIn is a platform for creating a Personal Brand, and in my opinion anyone who uses the term 'Personal Brand' should be told to go fuck themselves. Sideways.

Let's talk about your Personal Brand though.

I know, I know. I said it. Screw you – I'm the one writing this. I can say what I like.

OK.

What should a LinkedIn profile look like?

The photo is the first thing that people see when they see your profile. Please use a business-level photo for your profile: no pics of you with your cleavage out (gentlemen - you know who you are!)

or on nights out with your friends. This is the first place that many employers look and if you look like a third-rate porn star with 'hungry eyes' (again gentlemen - you know who you are!) then you can bet your last dollar that you will not be getting that phone call. Go for a professional looking shot that shows you as you are now not 10 years ago – a headshot or similar is best.

Directly underneath your profile picture there is a line that you can customize to show what you do and it is my strongest advice is to put something that describes what you do rather than just a Job Title. Mine is currently as follows: "I place the leading talent in the Microsoft Cloud & UC space - Azure & O365, Skype for Business" and I have changed it a couple of times over the past two years to reflect changes in the technology stack that I recruit for. To use the example of the iOS Developer above, it could read: "I design and build secure apps for the Enterprise using iOS, Azure, SSO and SWIFT." This strapline also features in the Search Engine of LinkedIn so it will pick up those keywords.

The next thing to look at is the Summary section of your Profile. Given that I actively want people to get in touch with me the first thing that my Summary section says is this:

"Connect with me on:

Mobile: (+44) 7957 355 228

DDI: (+44) 207 614 4423

Email: Will.Rowe@msemploy.co.uk"

Anyone who looks at my profile has all my contact details in one place and it is pretty much the first thing they see other than my obviously powerful profile picture. You will need to decide if you want people to be able to contact you directly or through the filter of LinkedIn InMails.

The positives are that you will be called more often about new roles. The negatives are that you will be called more often about new roles.

As in the Summary section of your résumé, it is important that you stay away from clichés and generic phrases and talk about what you do with detail and keywords that people might search on.

The next part of my Summary reads:

"I am a Recruitment Sales Director who is deeply passionate about the Microsoft Unified Communications and Cloud world covering Skype for Business, Azure and O365 technologies with experience recruiting at all levels from Engineer to Architect and Head of Practice / Partner.

Specialist in Executive Search and Contingency based recruitment techniques.

I have personally placed Microsoft Most Valuable Professionals (MVP), Microsoft Certified Masters and have an unparalleled network in this space.

Specialties: Microsoft and Wintel Server Technologies:

Skype for Business / Skype4B / Lync Online & O365, Lync 2013, Lync 2010, Migrations from OCS 2007

Lync Enterprise Voice, IM, Presence, Chat in Public Cloud, Hybrid and On-Premise engagements

MCSE, MCTS, MCiTP, MVP, MCM, MCSM, MCS

Public O365 Cloud and Private Cloud - Azure

Windows Core Infrastructure: 2008, 2012 R2, Active Directory

Exchange Server 2013 & Exchange Online"

There a lot of keywords in there obviously – the ones to look at are the repetitions across Skype & Lync, Cloud and Recruitment. They are in there several times and because I work extensively in this space I want to be found as easily as possible.

You could very easily cut and paste your newly optimized résumé into your profile and use this as the basis for getting found.

The thing with LinkedIn is that it is not enough anymore to just sit on there with a couple of hundred connections and wait for people to come to you. The platform is so huge now two things have happened:

It is harder to get found in amongst the 'noise' of other profiles.

It is easier than ever to find other like-minded people.

Once your profile is up to date and optimized you should start searching for people with similar skills to your own and ask them to connect with you. If you attend any industry events (and I'll talk more about this later) asking people who you have met there in real life to connect is a great way to increase your number of connections. Go to the Groups section, search for relevant discussion groups and you can join up to 50 of them: this will put in touch with the thought-leaders and industry up and comers who will posting in there.

Post some content yourself. Comment on things.

You could even write some articles and get some people discussing your opinions. My advice is pick a position which will inspire people to get involved: I wrote a piece entitled "Is the Skype for Business Consultant Role Dead?" and it got over 3,000 views and 30 odd comments. It is a great way to engage with your peers – you can also connect with them afterwards.

Why should you be doing this?

LinkedIn is not a job board. Recruiters are on it, and they will try to use it like a job board but the power of the platform is that if you connect with the right people, have opinions and can demonstrate your skills and experience through using the different features then you will be able to engage with hiring managers directly.

LinkedIn's main strength comes from giving you the ability to create a mini-following or tribe (for all you Seth Godin fans) for you and to give you a 'celebrity' status amongst your peers. Don't get me wrong – you will not suddenly be asked to the cool parties, but they are like way over-rated.

Or so I hear. People don't really ask me to them, and I'm usually quite busy anyways...

Anyhoo.

Link your LinkedIn profile to your GitHub / StackOverflow / blog and share your content with your connections. Invite people to give their thoughts on your thoughts, engage them in online and offline conversations, and you will be using the platform in the way that gives you the best return on your time.

This will take time though. You need to build your personal connections up – go for more than 500 as a starting point, and keep connecting.

Just remember: this is a social platform. Try interacting with people by commenting on their posts but please please please be a normal person. Be yourself. Comment for the sake of your thoughts not just to push your obvious excellence. Don't be a dick and be that person who uses the platform for negative bashing of other people.

Everything that you are doing will impact how people view you and the brand that you are building.

Twitter

This also applies to Twitter.

Everything you like or comment on is in the public eye. People you follow, things you 'like' or retweet.

I have personally rejected people from working for me because of the following on their (open and very easily found) Twitter feeds:

- Anti-Semitism
- Nudity
- Drugs:
  - Pictures
  - References to using drugs
  - #spliffsunday
- Swearing (references to the following)
  - F*ck
  - C**T
  - F*ckWomble
  - W*nkPuffin
  - N$*g£@
- Racism

Now - what do YOU have on Twitter, Facebook or Instagram? Would your grandmother be happy to see it? Or your children? That is the level you need to work at.

Twitter for me was a revelation when I finally 'got it'. I was merrily posting things and hoping that people might like them and then I started following the visible names in the industry I work. I started reading what they were tweeting about, and although much of it was (and indeed still is!) too technical for me to understand I began sharing it with my followers who in turn began to share that with their followers.

But I still didn't get it. Not really.

Twitter is about interacting and having conversations. If you are just retweeting other people's posts and hoping that someone will follow you then you must be a bit more proactive.

As with LinkedIn have a look at your profile and ask yourself what it says about you? Cleavage and hungry eyes? Hmmm – I think you know what you have to do.

One thing I would say is that Twitter is slightly more informal – if LinkedIn is for business then Twitter is more aimed at your internal stream of consciousness. Be yourself, use a more personal photo but don't be afraid to show a bit more of your quirky and beautiful personality. For your profile you should put in a couple of those all-important SEO-able terms we have been mentioning – use hashtags that are relevant but please don't put every word in a hashtag: it looks terrible and will put people off.

If you don't know what a hashtag is then Google it as there are many better sources of information for that than here.

The trick is to follow as many people who are relevant to your industry or sector as possible. I am, at the point of writing this, following 1548 people and have 632 followers of my @MSFTrecruit account and I would say that nearly every single one is a Microsoft specialist of some type. That is not a lot of followers in the grand scheme of things but it is something that I am actually very proud of: I don't want vast numbers irrelevant people clogging up my following. When I tweet something relevant I like to know that it generally will be seen by people who will be interested.

Many of my best placements have come from Direct Messages begun on Twitter where I have reached out to someone who is following me and engaged with them.

I now know how to put an amusing gif on a tweet – usually about penguins, weirdly. Blame @chrisovett for that. Follow him. He is occasionally very funny.

Twitter lets me engage with people directly and so you can as well. If you follow someone who is in your industry and they follow you back, send them a Direct Message introducing yourself. Don't try and sell them something, be yourself and be interested in them.

Reach out and try to start a discussion. See what happens if you start talking with a person who is a specialist in your field working at a company you might like to work for.

Rule 7: Evolve from just Online

Online is never as powerful as Offline

What I have found with all of these online platforms is that they are very powerful if used in the right way. What they will never be able to do act as a substitute for real-world offline meetings when you are looking at creating connections that will bear fruit in the future for your job search.

When did you last attend a User Group / Meet Up or an industry Expo? About two years ago I started attending four User Groups up and down the country and it has changed the way that I work and engage with people to such an extent that I wish I had done this ten years ago.

At first I was nervous of walking into a room full of Microsoft specialists who I didn't know and so to get over this I decided to speak with the organizers and ask them whether I might actually present at the next one.

This arranged, I turned up with memory stick in hand for what was one of the toughest presentations I have ever done. There were about 70 people present, I was ignored by half of the room who took the opportunity to grab some pizza, and the remainder who were watching seemed to take a sadistic pleasure in seeing me squirm during the section where in my naiveté I had thought that there might be some audience participation.

It didn't go well and the sound of that lone pitying laugh still haunts me in the wee small hours of the night.

The good thing is that you don't need to turn up and present at one of these meetups. What you can do is go and see some very interesting content from some of the thought leaders in your industry or sector, and be sitting in a room of likeminded people who all do a similar thing to you.

And guess what? They will all be on Twitter and LinkedIn. And they will be meeting you. And you can connect with them and follow them and start having meaningful real-life interactions with them.

What does this have to do with finding a new role?

The more people you meet in your space, the more people will know who you are. The more people who know who you are (particularly people in your industry) the more you will be considered for a new job without having to do anything.

LET'S GET BACK TO RAY.

If you recall, Ray was stuck in a Career Cul-de-Sac. His technical skills were out of date, and he was part of the furniture at his employer.

That employer was subsequently acquired by a much larger company and he was made redundant. He spent 6 months looking for a new role and this coincided with the arrival of his daughter, a beautiful little girl who really didn't enjoy sleeping all that much!

Ray became a stay at home Dad, perhaps the most important job that anyone can have, while his partner worked in the Medical and Healthcare industry.

Three and a half years later we were talking about how he could get back into employment, and I was of the opinion that he might make a good Recruitment Consultant finding people in the Project Management space. Ray came to work with me for a year, spending the first 3-6 months 'shaking the rust off' (i.e. being shouted at on a daily basis by me until he finally realized that he actually should do it my way rather than trying to make things up himself) and then not being too bad at the job.

His heart wasn't in it though.

It was at this point that one of my clients called me and asked me to find a specific type of person: not to find a set of skills but to find a person who had a totally customer-centric approach, who could talk with clients, and who might be able to do some business analysis followed by user adoption and training in the Microsoft Unified Communications space.

The first person I thought of was Ray.

We discussed it, and decided to get him into the process.

Before we did this, we worked on his résumé. Ray did a Brain Dump of everything he had done previously as a Support Manager with a focus on training, user adoption, business analysis and customer service. He used the Silos of Information technique to do this and we pulled across some of the new elements he had learned as a Recruiter: account management and sales.

As such, a résumé that probably shouldn't have matched too much on the face of it brought out the most relevant skills and the Director was very interested in meeting with him. Ray interviewed several times, and his passion for the role was such that even though he didn't have the right technical background he was eventually hired.

It was a steep learning curve for Ray and he worked hard in his new role, traveling up and down country and frequently staying away from home. His employer was acquired after two years in the role, and he called me to discuss his options as the company was haemorrhaging staff.

We discussed it, and agreed that he should attend a Unified Communications User Group in London with me, whereupon I introduced him to a few people that I know who work for a leading UC company I don't recruit for. They were interested to meet him but weren't hiring at the time.

A few months later he attended another one on his own, met up with the same guys again and they happened to be hiring.

A few introductions later Ray was interviewing through his own contacts and has subsequently started working for arguably the world's leading Microsoft Skype for Business consultancy as a User Adoption Specialist.

Ray has gone, in the space of 3 years, from a stay at home Dad who hadn't worked for 4 years to working for one of the top companies globally in a new field and I couldn't be happier, especially since he was able to broker the last move on his own with only a little advice from side-lines.

RULE 8: EVOLVE AND WORK WITH RECRUITERS

The recruitment world is a strange one. All too often we find we are tolerated as at best a necessary evil by many people, through to downright loathing. Occasionally you will come across someone who enjoys a good relationship with 'their' recruiter, but this is not the norm if you believe social media.

It is a sad, sad state of affairs that this is the case.

The challenges that we face as an industry are that we are unregulated, anyone with a suit and a pulse (and not necessarily in that order!) can do the job with no training or development prior to this and most of the recruitment companies in the world have less than 10 staff in them, usually less than 5. This means you have lots of small independent operators who often have little in the way of process to the way they work.

The majority of recruiters work on a contingency basis with their customers, meaning that if they do not fill the role they do not get paid. Most employers operate a preferred list of agencies so they will have anywhere between 3 and sometimes 20 agencies all fighting to fill the role. All the recruiters are fighting to find the right person and corners do sometimes get cut in these situations.

Let me stress though: for every negative thing you hear there are a dozen good experiences going unreported. Recruiters work hard, do long hours and if dealt with in the right way will usually go the extra mile for you.

As a candidate for a new role you will have to deal with a recruiter at some point.

What a recruiter wishes to know is:

- Are your skills and experience suitable for the role?
- Are your requirements in line with new role (is it a fit for you?)
- Do your salary / rate requirements align with what the role is paying?
- Are your communication skills strong enough for the role?
- Are they comfortable putting you in front of their customer?
- Do they feel that you will turn up to the interview, and are you reliable?

That's it. No more; no less.

This is the start of the interview process and regardless of your thoughts on Recruiters you need to treat it as such.

Be polite, friendly, and answer their questions in as much detail as possible.

If the role they are discussing isn't right for you, explain why and tell them what you do want.

Rule 9: Evolve and (W)Interview

If ever there was a flawed process for finding someone for a job, it is the interview process.

Seriously: 2-3 hours of meetings with someone to determine their fit for a new role which might encompass the next 3 years of their life? No wonder it still goes wrong so often.

I am not going to write a huge amount on interviewing. There are many books and video tutorials on the net currently that can give you deep insight into this (try a simple search on "Interview Tips Youtube" – there is a shed load on there alone!)

I simply want you think about the interview and ask yourself what you need to do to Win the Interview... or Winterview... I know – genius!

Consider it in the same terms as you did your résumé: the purpose of your interview is to sell yourself effectively. Given what we have looked at earlier hopefully you will be clearer on what you need to discuss with an interviewer.

If not, let us recap:

Selling = Identify what someone wants + Deliver it.

You will know what the requirements of the role are in advance of the meeting. If you are unclear ask your Recruiter or Talent person who is handling the role. If you don't have one reread the Job Description with an eye for what the requirements are.

These are what you need to tailor your experience to. If the requirements are for a VMware Architect with specific skills in vCloud Director, then that should be the first thing out of your mouth when the interviewer says, "Tell me about yourself..."

This new rule of interviewing is not in fact new: this is as old as it gets. You need to be clear on what the person sat opposite you needs to hear to make a decision, and then deliver it in the form of clear statements and examples that match their requirements.

"I am a Technical Architect who has been working with VMware since v.x and recently I've been designing cloud based platforms with vCloud Director..."

Let us not forget though that an interview is a two-way street.

Before going in, get out your Ideal Job Description Template and revisit it. What did you write in there that was important to you, and what does that ideal role look like?

Use this as the basis for building a set of questions for the interviewer to answer and then take them in with you. Asking questions is one of the most important parts of the process for you: what do you need to get answered before you are in a position to decide if the role is right for you?

Does the culture fit with your requirements around how you want to be treated (does it align with your Values?)

Is the training / environment / work on offer going to give you the chance to stay current with the industry, or are you going to be needing to take action in 6-12 months after your next Career Audit?

What is the career path, and what will you need to do to get that next promotion / a sexier role?

Rule 10: Evolve or Die

With that we reach the end of this voyage into the new rules for you IT career and for finding a job in the IT space. I hope that this has given you food for thought and that you will implement the ideas. This takes time and often it will make you ask some tough questions.

That is a good thing.

We work in an industry which is evolving constantly with new products and sectors coming to the market in an ever-shortening timescale, and there has never been a more exciting time to be a part of it. Your job is no longer the day-to-day work you get paid for: now it is to evolve with the market and always be considering how to do so.

To recap:

- Rule 1: Being Happy isn't enough to Evolve.
- Rule 2: Evolve through a Career Audit.
- Rule 3: Evolve by knowing what you want.
- Rule 4: Evolve and be found.
- Rule 5: Evolve and Sell.
- Rule 6: Evolve your Brand
- Rule 7: Evolve from just Online
- Rule 8: Evolve and work with Recruiters
- Rule 9: Evolve and (W)Interview
- Rule 10: Evolve or Die

The rules have changed.

Evolve or Die, my friend.

EVOLVE OR DIE.

About The Author

Will Rowe has worked in the IT Recruitment space since 1999 and focuses primarily on the Microsoft world. He is a recruitment trainer as well as continuing to find awesome people awesome jobs.

He lives in the United Kingdom in Kent, the Garden of England, with his wife Hannah and son Joshua, and when not engaged in recruitment and tech matters can be found creating weird and wonderful jams in the kitchen.

ONE LAST THING...

If you enjoyed this book or found it useful I'd be very grateful if you'd post a short review on Amazon. Your support really does make a difference and I read all the reviews personally so I can get your feedback and make this book even better.

If you'd like to leave a review then all you need to do is click the review link on this book's page on Amazon here: http://amzn.to/yourlink (direct link to the "Create a review" page on Amazon for your book – you can't get the link until you upload your book first. Then, when your book is live, go get the link, insert it, and re-upload your book.)

Thanks again for your support!

Printed in Great Britain
by Amazon

29193526R00040